THE MERCHANT NAVY

Richard Woodman

SHIRE PUBLICATIONS

Published in Great Britain in 2013 by Shire Publications Ltd, Midland House, West Way, Botley, Oxford OX2 0PH, United Kingdom.

4301 21st St, Suite 220B, Long Island City, NY 11101, USA.

E-mail: shire@shirebooks.co.uk   www.shirebooks.co.uk

A CIP catalogue record for this book is available from the British Library.

Shire Library no. 736.   ISBN-13: 978 0 74781 232 6

Richard Woodman has asserted his right under the Copyright, Designs and Patents Act, 1988, to be identified as the author of this book.

Designed by Tony Truscott Designs, Sussex, UK and typeset in Perpetua and Gill Sans.

Printed in China through Worldprint Ltd.

13 14 15 16 17   10 9 8 7 6 5 4 3 2 1

COVER IMAGE
The size and variety of the British merchant fleet is shown here in this public information image produced during the Second World War. (Imperial War Museum image PST 014011.)

TITLE PAGE IMAGE
A British poster of the Second World War expressing the nation's gratitude to the Merchant Navy for delivering food and vital supplies. Two merchant seamen fire an anti-aircraft gun during the Battle of the Atlantic. In the background flies the red ensign – the flag of the Merchant Navy.

CONTENTS PAGE IMAGE
The famous clipper race, between the *Ariel* and *Taeping* in 1866, bringing back tea from China to London. Clippers were built for speed and before the opening of the Suez Canal there was an annual clipper race. The winners earned a bonus for the first tea cargo delivered.

IMAGE ACKNOWLEDGEMENTS
Alamy, page 36; Author's collection, page 19 (top), 33 (bottom), 47 (bottom); © Courtesy of the British Mercantile Marine Memorial Collection, page 26; Courtesy of Ambrose Greenaway, page 50; Robert Hunter, pages 37 (bottom), 49 (bottom); John Morris, page 52; The Honourable Company of Master-Mariners, page 20; Mary Evans Picture Library, page 28; National Maritime Museum, page 23 (top); Private Collection, page 49 (top); Louis Roskell, page 48. All other images are courtesy of Peter Newark's Historical Pictures.

Shire Publications is supporting the Woodland Trust, the UK's leading woodland conservation charity, by funding the dedication of trees.

CONTENTS

WHAT IS THE MERCHANT NAVY?

MARITIME NATIONS are defined by their possession of a navy and a mercantile marine, the first consisting of their armed ships of war, the second of privately owned vessels that carry cargoes for profit either in the national interest, as imports and exports, or on behalf of others. Such national commercial 'fleets' are commonly referred to as a 'mercantile marine,' but in Britain it is known as the 'Merchant Navy' as a result of its importance and extraordinary sacrifice in the First World War. This was repeated between 1939 and 1945 when the integration of merchant shipping with the armed forces was so close that it did, in fact, become a second 'navy,' all ships being armed. The ships of national mercantile marines 'wear' the maritime ensign of the country in which they are registered and by which they are regulated; the ships of the British Merchant Navy wear the red ensign. Although initially also a naval ensign, an Act of Parliament in 1864 had made this the exclusive flag of privately owned British vessels.

Historically, the private ownership of vessels has been vested in a wide range of commercial entities. Some possessed no more than perhaps one or two vessels of a single type; others comprised huge and complex conglomerates with scores of ships designed with different purposes in mind and trading all over the globe under a variety of company names. Today the British Merchant Navy includes not only ships owned by British citizens, but also those placed by their owners under British regulation under the Tonnage Tax regime. This entitles them to wear the red ensign of Great Britain and, in exchange for certain undertakings (chief of which is the training of young seafarers) to receive tax breaks. British registry implies their owners sign-up to certain audited practices, which range from safety and maintenance standards to the protection of the environment through on-board regulation. This assurance of quality allows an owner of a British registered ship to be placed on the so-called 'white list' of national registers, making his vessels more attractive to those seeking safe and profitable delivery of their cargoes. Owning a British-registered vessel also guarantees the protection of the Royal Navy in troubled times.

Opposite:
Tudor sailors like this, most likely civilian crewmen for merchant vessels, often found themselves involved in sea battles as England and Spain fought for control of the great Atlantic sea routes.

HOW IT ALL BEGAN

The origins of both the British Merchant and Royal Navies lie in the first half of the sixteenth century when, under Henry VIII, England in particular began to flex her muscles as a potential maritime power. There had been an early medieval trade with western France (then mostly fiefdoms of the Norman kings of England), wine being the most important import. It was loaded in Bordeaux in large casks, or 'tuns', from which we derive the expression for describing a ship's capacity, or 'burthen.' This system of measurement facilitated both the levying of the king's customs duties and the value of a vessel when requisitioned for war. Growing exports of English wool for manufacture into cloth in Flanders encouraged trade on the east coast of England, but much commerce at the time was borne not in English ships but in those of the Hanseatic League – a confederation of the mercantile associations of port-states in what is now modern Germany – which established commercial bases in places as far apart as Bergen (in Norway) and London. These 'easterlings' became renowned for their straight-dealing, from which is derived the word 'sterling' as a mark of the soundness of the British national currency. With much of our trade in the hands of foreigners, there was little call for any major home-grown enterprise until the reign of Richard II (1377–99), when this became a political issue. In 1381 the first

Merchant ships during the reign of Edward IV in the late fifteenth century. The first Navigation Act of 1381 had already forbidden the export of cargo in anything other than an English vessel, encouraging the growth of privately owned merchant ships.

'Navigation Act' forbade the export of cargo in anything other than an English vessel, encouraging the growth of small ship-owning syndicates of English merchants.

Besides the wine and wool trades, English, Irish, Welsh and Scottish coastal communities had begun to extend their fishing further offshore. Meanwhile, coal began to be mined in the north-east of England, which answered a demand being created in the slow but steady expansion of London; this created a coastal coal trade that would last until the second half of the twentieth century. Despite all this, English commercial shipping remained limited in its ambitions, largely coastal or cross-Channel, extended further only by overseas military adventures. The English and Scots remained island peoples, their kings fighting each other and feuding with their nobles, their respective homelands being regarded by much of Europe as *ultima Thule*.

It was not until the dynastic Wars of the Roses finally ended in 1485 that the incoming Tudors offered England the conditions under which the initiative of its merchants might truly prosper. By this time there were rumours of far-off countries of fabulous wealth. Hearing of Columbus's discoveries in 1492, and encouraged by London's merchants, Henry VII employed the Genoese navigator Giovanni Caboto (John Cabotto) to 'discover' a territory in this 'New World' for England. In 1486 Cabot laid claim to what

Yorkshire-born Sir Martin Frobisher was a merchant venturer who explored the possibility of a north-west passage for trade to China for the Company of Cathay in 1577. Here, he encounters hostile Inuit.

he called 'Newfoundland' and, on their homeward voyage, Cabot and his crew aboard the *Matthew* came across the cod-rich waters of the Grand Bank. From this point Englishmen began to look to seaward to make their fortunes while simultaneously competing with the Portuguese, who also fished the Grand Bank.

Henry VIII succeeded his father in 1509; he was young and ambitious. His break with Rome over his divorce from Catherine of Aragon brought England into conflict with a Catholic Europe, itself riven by the new Protestantism. Fired by an energetic zeal purporting to be Protestant but not unmixed with envy and opportunism, an increasing number of young men went to sea in search of plunder. They actively defied the Papal decree that divided the world between the dominant maritime nations of Spain and Portugal. Riches poured into the coffers of Madrid and Lisbon, largely from the import of silver from Peru and the highly prized spices from islands in the distant east. To an aggressive Protestant state the Papal ruling was a

In this woodcut of 1580, English wine merchants from Newcastle, Bristol and London buy wine in Bordeaux, France, to ship back to England.

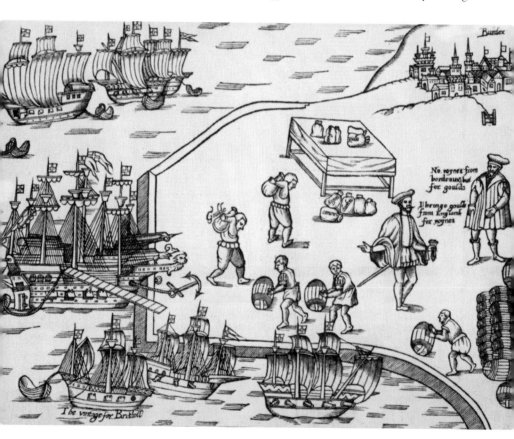

8

challenge and English mariners and their backers sought to break this cartel. These 'merchant venturers' came chiefly from the emerging middle class but were joined by a small number of aristocrats. Chiefly based in Bristol and London, these syndicates sent out speculative trading expeditions financed by joint stock companies, which avoided direct confrontation with the predominating maritime powers by attempting to out-flank them. One tried to find a route to the Spice Islands to take advantage of the high prices commanded by nutmeg in particular, but the chosen route to the Orient, north of Russia and through the north-east passage, was barred by ice. The first voyage commanded by Sir Hugh Willoughby ended in disaster in 1554, notwithstanding which the Muscovy Company opened a profitable trade with Russia. Joined by the Levant Company, which concentrated on trade with the eastern Mediterranean, these two joint stock companies laid the foundation of regular English overseas commerce in English ships, the latter founding overseas consulates. Attempts to reach the east by way of the north-west passage, though preoccupying explorers for far too long, also ended in disaster but, in the final years of the reign of Queen Elizabeth I (who secretly invested in the enterprise), a group of London merchants and investors were granted a royal charter incorporating them as the East India Company. It was thi commercial venture, led by James Lancaster, which laid the foundations of the British Raj in India.

Other trades flourished during the intermittent wars with Spain that bedevilled much of Elizabeth's reign. The English slave trade brought John Hawkins and Francis Drake to public notice in the early 1560s and their

Sir Francis Drake was a slave trader and privateer who became famous for his voyages of exploration. His merchant ships were available to the monarch as men-of-war when required.

Ark Royal, flagship of Lord Howard, fighting the Spanish Armada in 1588. Many merchant vessels formed the fleet that stopped the threatened Spanish invasion of England.

ships were available to the monarch as men-of-war when required. Thus, in the sixteenth century, the expression 'Navy Royal' comprised all the ships in the kingdom and it was this hybrid force that defeated the Spanish Armada in 1588. It was now that religious intolerance and naked ambition encouraged overseas settlement in North America, all of which was supported by a growing body of English shipping. Transatlantic trade continued during the English Civil Wars, while the Commonwealth government and Protectorate under Cromwell in the middle of the seventeenth century did much to improve the English navy as it fought the Dutch. It further empowered merchant shipping by the passing of another Navigation Act in 1651. This strengthened the hold of national shipping on trade with the North

Admiral Robert Blake engages a Dutch warship in 1653, one of a series of wars against the Netherlands that determined English maritime dominance of the sea. Note the red ensign flying from the rear of the English ship on the left – in Blake's day this flag was used by both men-of-war and merchant ships.

American colonies, to which, as a consequence of the foreign policy of Oliver Cromwell, the sugar-growing island of Jamaica was added in 1655. After his Restoration, Charles II passed further Navigation Acts in 1660, 1663 and 1672. This last, which precipitated the Third Dutch War, effectively destroyed the Dutch navy and left the way clear for the expansion of English merchant shipping, particularly that of the East India Company in the Indian and China Seas.

By the end of the seventeenth century, Scotland was also seeking similar overseas success but Scottish ventures, particularly that at Dairen in central America, failed disastrously, almost bankrupted the country and led directly to the Act of Union with England in 1707. Like England, Scotland had opened a commerce with Russia by way of the White Sea and the Baltic, and both countries traded with Scandinavia. It was from these northern nations that Great Britain imported commodities such as iron, turpentine, rosin, flax, hemp, oak and pine – all of which were essential to shipping, both commercial and naval, and collectively known as 'naval stores'.

Investors in the South Sea Company, facilitating mercantile marine trade with South America, lose their money when the 'bubble' bursts in the City of London in 1720.

Economic success on the plantations in Jamaica and southern colonies of North America increased the use of slave labour in English as well as Spanish colonies, attracting investment from the merchants of Liverpool, but the slave trade was given its greatest boost by the 'Peace of Utrecht' of 1713. This ended the War of Spanish Succession and, during the negotiations, the British diplomats wrung from Spain the permanent occupation of Gibraltar and the monopoly to carry slaves to the Caribbean – known as the '*Asiento des negros*'. (The *Asiento* reverted to Spain in 1750 on payment of £100,000.) The government awarded the *Asiento* to another joint stock enterprise, the South Sea Company, which had been formed in 1711 to facilitate trade with South America and to rival both the East India Company and the newly established Bank of England. Backed by the Treasury, it was more a political instrument than a *bona fide* trading enterprise. By 1720 the company's plan to take over the national debt led to a speculative boom that went ballistic in what was called the 'South Sea Bubble.' Most investors, including King George I, lost heavily, many being forced into exile or driven to suicide. None of this greatly affected the shipping boom occasioned by the slave trade, which prospered until much later in the century when humanitarian agitation began to turn public opinion against it.

SHIP OWNERS, MARINERS AND SEAMEN

From the earliest times, ship owning and seafaring had been a precarious and uncertain business, hence the notion of a voyage being known as a 'venture'. Such were the dangers that no single owner took up the challenge, risk being spread by dividing the ownership of a vessel into sixty-fourths. Even a wealthy merchant would be unlikely to own more than a handful of shares in any one ship, though he might invest in a number thereof, while the system allowed small investors a chance of a profit. Slowly groups of syndics emerged outside the more formalised joint stock companies, often specialising in certain trades and including the men actually in command of merchant ships, their 'master-mariners'.

Since the purpose of a merchant ship was to make money, the selection of a master was usually to promote the commercial success of her voyage and he was not necessarily an accomplished seaman or navigator. It was often better for a syndicate to employ one of their fellow shareholders, or a relative, to take charge, leaving the mundane tasks of handling a vessel to the second-in-command, better known as 'the mate'. Essentially an inefficient system leading to a good deal of shipwreck, it was accepted for many years in the absence of anything better.

Mates, and there was usually more than one as it was necessary to maintain a constant watch, were customarily drawn from the more intelligent seamen. The senior was invariably known as *the* mate, his junior the second mate, and so forth. Certain trades (most notably the colliers hauling coal on the east coast of England, or similar vessels that plied to the Baltic and north Russia, and the whalers that ventured into the Arctic to hunt the bowhead-whale) operated an indentured apprenticeship for boys, but little navigation was taught; although it was considered the way to becoming a mate, it was still a truly primitive art. The East India Company, like the Royal Navy, took a more professional view, not least because their ships were exponentially more valuable than ordinary merchantmen, but also because they made long voyages out of sight of land. As in men-of-war, it was common in these vessels to find young men of good family serving as midshipmen – proto-officers – the Company requiring up to six mates in the largest of their Indiamen. These, by the middle of the eighteenth century, measured up to 800 tons burthen.

Life for most of these men was tough, but it was harsher still for the ordinary seamen. Employed entirely for their physical energy, fed and paid the barest minimum, they were a much put-upon breed. In the days before tinned food and preserved fresh water, their diet was limited largely to salt meat and other dried provisions. The Vitamin C deficiency known as scurvy was prevalent and, although James Lancaster had known about the restorative effect of fresh fruit when it was available, there was great resistance to both the promulgation and the acceptance of this remedy. Seafaring was not a life of choice; more that of economic necessity. In times of dire need, particularly in the early seventeenth century, merchant sailors turned readily to piracy, while the tough conditions they were obliged to endure could, and did, prime them for mutiny. Even if they escaped shipwreck, diseases and accidents – the most usual being rupture – were common. However, despite these obstacles, it was possible for an intelligent seaman, if he was fortunate and applied himself, to rise in the service and the British mercantile marine was always a meritocracy.

An English sailor of 1650 stands ready to defend his ship against Spanish or Dutch commercial rivals.

BRITAIN RULES THE WAVES

D ESPITE THE LOSS of the American Colonies in 1783, Britain's wars with France and Spain during the eighteenth century had seen the growth of a maritime empire which included Canada, an increasing number of islands in the West Indies, large tracts of India and, thanks to the explorations of James Cook, a knowledge of the existence of Australia and New Zealand. Besides taking over the government of much of the Indian sub-continent and encouraging the expansion of the three great cities of Bombay (Mumbai), Madras (Chennai) and Calcutta (Kolkotta), the East India Company's surveyors had also greatly added to the knowledge of the navigable waters of the world, the Company's ships extending its trade-routes to China and even the remote and isolated empire of Japan.

THE GREAT WAR WITH FRANCE, 1793–1815

Although American independence created a new mercantile marine which would in time become a serious competitor to the British, the post-war resumption of transatlantic trade was swift. Close ties and commercial imperatives quickly healed the political schism. It was the political upheaval of the French Revolution of 1789 that confronted Britain with a real danger, precipitating a new war in 1793. Except for a short truce between 1802 and 1803, hostilities would engulf much of the world until the defeat of Napoleonic France at Waterloo in June 1815. For Great Britain, the consequences of the final victory over the French – by no means certain in 1802 – were momentous. The Battle of Trafalgar in October 1805 was an important victory, but it did not end the war at sea. Nelson's triumph enabled the Royal Navy to counter the sea-power of the enemy which, though vigorously active against British trade for a further decade, was never actually sufficient to interrupt it.

Napoleon's 'Continental System', which was designed to shut the British out of all traffic with Europe and thereby ruin a 'nation of shop-keepers', back-fired. Thanks to British enterprise and a convoy system protected by the Royal Navy, between 1793 and 1815 British merchant shipping doubled

Opposite: Poster for Cunard Line, advertising the *Carmania* and *Caronia* passenger steamships en route from Liverpool to New York and Boston, c. 1910.

Captain James
Cook lands in
Australia. It was
British naval
explorers like
Cook who added
greatly to the
knowledge of the
globe and helped
British merchant
shipping establish
trade routes all
around the world.

in tonnage. This in turn led to improvements in ports, most notably in London where a rapidly expanded wet-dock system displaced the old river berths where ships were vulnerable to pilfering and grounding. Smaller dock complexes were built elsewhere, though Liverpool's was as extensive as the capital's. During the next century, London would grow to become

Although the
battle of Trafalgar
in 1805 was an
important victory,
it was Britain's
merchant shipping
that managed
to defeat
Napoleon's
blockade
of Europe.

the world's largest port, with Liverpool, Glasgow, Hull, the Tyne and the ports of the Bristol Channel also handling vast quantities of cargo.

British merchant shipping had played a vital, though unappreciated, part in the defeat of Napoleon. By maintaining the flow of commodities Britain had been able to grow her economy, subsidise her allies, supply her overseas armies (especially Wellington's in the Iberian peninsula) and exert her influence worldwide. This

Sailors of the late eighteenth century. These were the seamen who helped crew the convoys of merchant shipping and warships that eventually defeated Napoleon in his attempt to dominate the sea.

achievement was enabled and over-shadowed by the projection of political sea-power by the Royal Navy which, in a nation rapidly enriched by industry and overseas trade, was able to expand as it embraced new technology. This augmentation of naval power-projection created conditions in which Great Britain was able to dominate the century between Waterloo and the outbreak of the First World War, making her the modern world's first super-power.

PAX BRITANNICA

Although other countries such as the United States, Germany, Italy and, towards the end of the nineteenth century, Japan steadily increased their

Great Western, a steamship designed by Brunel and completed in Bristol in 1837. British maritime technology advanced rapidly in the nineteenth century and increased the volume of long-distance voyages.

STEAM SHIP "GREAT WESTERN,"
1340 tons Burthen,
Lieut. James Hosken, R. N., Commander.
BETWEEN NEW YORK & BRISTOL.

In consequence of pressing solicitations from a number of passengers and merchants, the sailing days of the above ship have been altered, and she is now appointed to sail for the present year, as follows:—

From Bristol.	*From New-York.*
Saturday 19th Jan 1839.	Wed'y. 13th Feb. 1839.
" 9th March "	" 13th April "
" 27th April "	" 22d May "
" 15th June "	" 10th July "
" 3d August "	" 28th August "
" 21st Sept. "	" 16th Oct "
" 9th Nov. "	" 4 h Dec. "

Fare to Bristol—In main Saloon, and cuddy state rooms, Thirty-Five Guineas; in fore and lower saloons, Thirty Guineas; steward's fees, *l*1,10; children under 13, and servants half price.
No second class or steerage passengers taken.
For passage or freight, apply to

RICHARD IRVIN, 98 Front street,
ja3 Agent of the Great Western Steam Ship Co

maritime muscle under this general *Pax Britannica*, by 1914 British merchantmen carried just under half the world's trade. This was due to a number of factors in which British shipping was the essential facilitator, exporting the goods made in what had become the manufactory of the world, providing mail and passenger services – particularly for the purposes of permanent emigration – to North America, South Africa, Australia and New Zealand. This in turn created new markets for British manufacturers, while investment in other parts of the world beyond the imperial pale also created demands for shipping services. These included South America and China and they were in turn cranked up by the development of the steamship, a technology which the British, with their reserves of coal and their expertise in shipbuilding, were able to exploit to the full. British inventiveness went further, moving from wooden to iron and later

This sailing notice, published in New York in 1839, lists the dates of *Great Western's* voyages from New York to Bristol.

The *Britannia*, first of the Cunard steamships, sailed from Liverpool to Boston on her maiden voyage in July 1840. Author Charles Dickens later sailed on her to America.

steel ships, enabling bigger vessels with improved engines to overcome the early disadvantages of steam. Bigger and more viable ships improved profits and prospects. Steamers could voyage successfully to China by 1866 and to Australia by 1881, both passages greatly helped by the opening of the Suez Canal in 1869. Britannia did indeed rule the waves.

Shipbuilding in iron and steel tended to move these industries north, where the sources of iron ore and coal were more readily to be found. On the banks of most rivers in Britain shipbuilding of one sort or another could be found; huge shipyards sprang up along the River Mersey, the Wear, the Tyne, the Clyde and at Queen's Island, Belfast. These yards built both merchantmen and men-of-war, not only for Britain, but for the world, an extraordinary accomplishment which would attract envy, particularly from Germany, but also from other countries such as the United States and Japan. The development in British ship design, held back by the Napoleonic War, had received a sharp shock from the post-war successes of fast new American sailing ships, a circumstance from which the short-lived tea clipper arose, but the American Civil War stalled progress and held the United States back for some years, leaving the field clear for the British.

An early nineteenth-century leadsman swings his lead line to take a sounding of the depth of the water in this illustration by George Cruikshank.

The Grand Saloon of a transatlantic passenger steamship of the 1860s. The vast boom in emigration from Britain to the rest of the world expanded overseas markets for British goods transported by the Merchant Navy.

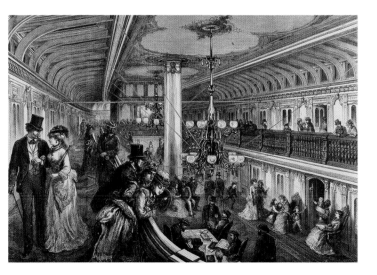

The tea clipper and the late nineteenth-century emigrant carrier brought the full-rigged ship to a state of near perfection. Here the *Harbinger* lies in the Thames with the 'Blue Peter' flying from her foremast head, indicating that her departure for Australia is imminent. Painting by J. Spurling.

The composition of the British merchant fleet during this era became increasingly varied. After competition with American clippers had brought the full-rigged sailing ship to a state of near perfection with the beautiful tea clipper (of which the remaining survivor, the *Cutty Sark*, may be seen today at Greenwich), sailing ships continued to be built to improving and larger designs into the twentieth century. Ironically, they benefited from the necessity of supplying reserves of fine quality Welsh 'steam coal' all over the world for the use of British merchant steamers and men-of-war. They were then able to seek out homogenous cargoes such as the annual Australian wool-clip, jute from Calcutta, or nitrate from Chile for their homeward lading; thus for about a century, steam and sail co-existed.

While the steamer had risen to global importance on the back of the desire of the British government to control its colonies and the essential mail contracts that ensured this – the first worldwide net – it was not long before another communications network was being put into place: that of the submarine telegraph cable. This was accomplished by a number of specially fitted out ships which laid thousands upon thousands of miles of insulated

Merchant marine steamers and sailing ships moored in George's Dock, Liverpool. Both forms of shipping operated side by side for much of the nineteenth century. Liverpool was a major international port during this period, receiving a large trade in cotton.

copper cable. This gave rise to subsidiary industries and necessary imports of copper and the gutta-percha used for insulation. While a dedicated cable-layer was developed for the purpose, early pioneering work had been carried out by the world's largest auxiliary steamship, the *Great Eastern*, which was otherwise a flop. Once established, the submarine telegraph network provided commerce as well as government with a new management tool, improving the information flow and allowing all manner of heightened sophistication in the way business – and in particular shipping – was carried out.

By about 1890, however, a cheap form of steam vessel known as the 'tramp' had been developed. The tramp steamer could be run almost as cheaply as

The Royal Mail Line's steamship *Europa*, carrying a combination of mail, passengers and freight. Before the laying of the first transatlantic cable in 1858, mail ships were the only form of communication between Britain and the rest of the world.

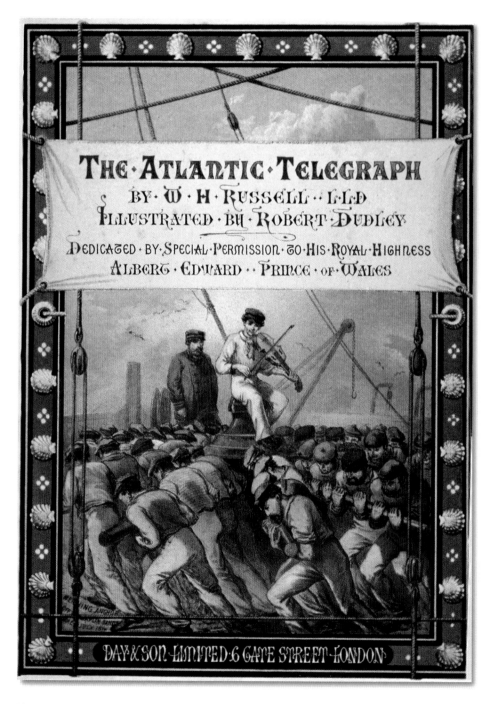

a sailing vessel and in due course would supersede her. A tramp steamer was not delayed by contrary winds and could react to the spot-markets as well as carting homogenous cargoes all over the world.

The steam-powered ship had now come of age, dispensing with her auxiliary masts and sails. The early development of steam had proved expensive; the so-called 'steam-navigation companies' seeking to profit from the new technology struggled without securing a lucrative government mail contract to underwrite their expenses. The installation of steam machinery and boilers, plus the additional space required for bunkers and the expense of engineers and firemen, were a heavy burden to which had to be added the cost of fuel. The retention of sails until the 1880s was a necessary precaution, not least because propeller shafts often broke, but innovation and refinement rapidly improved ship construction so that large transatlantic passenger liners were commonplace by the end of the century.

Similarly, smaller cargo liners, many of which carried a limited number of passengers, were able to carry a huge variety of manufactured goods – what were called 'general cargoes' – on scheduled services. Such ships formed the backbone of the British carrying fleet that bore half the world's commerce, operating from Archangel in the north to Ushaia in the south and from Yokohama in the east to Vancouver in the west. Many did not visit the United Kingdom at all, but left their shipyards to maintain a 'cross-trade' between India and South Africa, or between Japan and Australia, or China and the United States. Companies grew up to specialise in particular trades, or in the carriage of particular items. As an example of the former, the Pacific Steam Navigation Company traded between Europe and South America; as an example of the latter, Cayzer, Irvine's Clan Line delivered most of the locomotives and rolling stock for the Indian railway network. Some shipping firms grew from other enterprises, expanding the activities of the original organisation, the best example of which were the magnificent passenger liners of the Canadian Pacific Railway Company.

Shipping companies adopted distinctive colour schemes, or 'liveries', consisting of unique hull, mast and funnel colours, with refinements carried as far as the paint schemes inside ventilators, coupling this with their own system of naming ships. Obviously those of the Clan Line were named after

A fireman tends the coal-fired boiler on a steamship. A network of good supplies of fine-quality Welsh 'steam coal' was needed all around the globe to maintain steamship routes. The supply of this coal was another task for the Merchant Navy.

Opposite: Merchant seamen helping to lay the Atlantic telegraph cable from the deck of the *Great Eastern*, as depicted on the title page of a book celebrating the achievement in 1863.

Above: This Castle Line booklet lists the passengers and crew of the *Tantallon Castle*, sailing from Cape Town to London in 1898. It also carried British colonial mail.

Scottish clans; the grand liners of the Canadian Pacific Railway Company were all Empresses. Others adopted prefixes or suffixes: the tramp ships of Hain's of St Ives in Cornwall all had names beginning with the Cornish '*Tre*', while all Cunarders – with the exception of the famous Queens – ended in '*ia*', such as the *Mauretania*; and all White Star liners in '*ic*', of which the most notorious must be the *Titanic*. There were many others: Scottish glens; various saints, kings and princes; artists, artisans and philosophers; countries, provinces and cities, even the halls of the country gentry. Some went to extremes: not content with naming their ships after Scottish mountains, those of the Ben Line of Leith sported steel deck-houses specially painted to appear as if panelled in wood. Such devices were a form of advertising, both at home and abroad, attracting not just passengers but the all-important shippers, whose produce and manufactures earned far more revenue as cargo than any number of passengers with their demands of food, accommodation and entertainment. To these individual motifs were added each company's house-flag, which might be merely the monogram of the original owner, as in the case of Alfred Holt's Blue Funnel Line, or the combined colours of the two royal houses of Spain and Portugal, as in the case of the Peninsular and Oriental Steam Navigation Company. Trading first to ports in the Iberian peninsula and proud of their mail contract (without which they would have got nowhere), Brodie Wilcox and Arthur Anderson, the founders of P&O, adopted the blue and white of the Braganzas of Portugal, with the red and gold of Castile and Aragon in a house-flag still in use today.

By the end of the First World War the commercial empire that Wilcox and Anderson founded had become a huge conglomerate under James Mackay, the first Lord Inchcape. Besides owning P&O, Inchcape's board directed the affairs of the British India Steam Navigation Company and half a dozen smaller shipping companies, including Hain of St Ives. In contrast were hundreds of medium- and smaller-sized enterprises. Indeed the great tramp-ship owning ports of South Wales and the north-east coast of England boasted scores of small firms, some owning only one or two ships. Many shipping companies divided their fleets up into much smaller separate units, often consisting of a single ship so that, for the purposes of taxes and accounting, their owners maximised profits and limited losses. British merchant ships operate on a voyage-by-voyage basis and damage to cargo through bad weather, even the wreck of the ship herself, could be isolated and not spread across the parent company's portfolio. Although huge profits could be generated from ship owning thanks to these devices and economies of scale, it was then (as now) nevertheless a business subject to global fluctuation, to wars, civil unrest and labour troubles, to the rise and fall in commodity prices and to fuel price-hikes. Profit lies in the margins, and ship owners – British as well as foreign – became adept at complex manipulations.

Loading wheat on sailing ships at Port Melbourne in Victoria, Australia. The invention of shipboard refrigeration in the late nineteenth century allowed the transport of meat as well as grain from Australia and New Zealand to Britain.

New innovation seemed to be everywhere, the appliance of science extending to new methods of transportation of protein. While the movement of carbohydrates such as grains and rice had long been undertaken by sea, few proteins could be shifted in sufficient bulk to influence world prices. Cheese and salt-fish were an exception, but they sold only to restricted markets. Salt meat had been the diet of seafarers for centuries, along with the scurvy that went with it, but the consequences of emigration to Australia and New Zealand resulted in huge sheep-stations, along with the beef-producing *estancias* of the pampas of South America, in which British investment played a large part. These produced vast quantities of meat for export to an industrialised urban population in Britain and Europe. To make this practicable required the development of refrigeration, first fitted to sailing ships in the late nineteenth century and later installed into steamers, many of which were soon loading entire cargoes of frozen mutton, lamb and beef. Like tea, the import of which in quantity from India had so reduced its price that it became a staple of British working people's life, cheap frozen meat greatly improved the national diet.

By the end of the nineteenth century yet another new factor had come into play, the influence of the internal combustion engine. While the steady increase in demand for materials such as rubber (recently transplanted from Brazil to Malaya by ship) could be coped with by the established shipping arrangements, oil as a portable fuel presented new problems. Oils of various sorts had been increasingly used and by the mid-nineteenth century the hitherto most common, whale oil, was being superseded by kerosene, or paraffin as the British called it. Widely used for heating, cooking and lighting, the use of kerosene rapidly increased. Meanwhile the growth in demand for other oils was stimulating prospecting in all corners of the world.

Mineral oils were originally raised from shale in the United States and when exported had been carried in barrels stowed in sailing ships, a high-risk and destructive cargo. Later, large sailing oil tankers were constructed, their hulls subdivided into deep tanks with auxiliary steam-pumps to handle the cargo. As oil reserves were discovered elsewhere, others began to take an interest, among them Marcus Samuel. Up to this point, Samuel had dealt in the import of exotic shells, largely from Borneo – hence the name of the company he founded. Sensing an expanding market for kerosene in the Far East, Samuel resolved to satisfy it by supplying the produce of the oil fields of Baku on the shores of the Caspian Sea. Aware that oil passing through the Suez Canal would have to comply with the stringent safety regulations imposed by the Anglo-French Suez Canal Company, Samuel ordered one of a new type of ship, an oil tanker. Samuel negotiated a consignment of 4,000

Marcus Samuel's purpose-designed oil tanker, *Murex*.

tons of kerosene and in 1882 had it loaded into his new British-built tanker, the *Murex*, named after a shell in which his company had once trafficked. The vessel was an immediate success. Discharged in a few hours, her steam plant cleaned her tanks so efficiently that she loaded a back-cargo of rice. A decade later Samuel owned eleven tankers and in 1897 the Shell Transport and Trading Company was born.

Samuel was almost alone in breaking into this new business. Although happy to load cargoes of oil in drums and tins in wooden cases – known as 'case-oil' – with one or two exceptions, British ship owners were wary of investing in these costly new vessels. Most of the companies owning oil tankers were off-shoots of the companies actually prospecting for, extracting and processing crude oil – the oil-majors of our own time. These were good examples of shipping enterprises which arose to extend and foster an independent business. Among the modern multi-nationals who found this necessary was what we know today as BP, whose British Tanker Company remains a carrier of crude oil and its derivatives.

A ship's wireless officer sends an SOS distress signal from a burning vessel. New communication technology helped improve navigation and shipboard safety at the beginning of the twentieth century.

In this way, in the century between 1815 and 1914, British merchant shipping had a profound influence upon the world in which we live. Whether it was the mass-migration of whole populations escaping the over-crowded industrial cities of Britain and intent on a better life in the Antipodes, the establishment of the first global communications network, the relief of chronic dietary deficiencies by the easier transport of foodstuffs, the feeding of industrial processes, or even the movement of troops to distant battlefields, all went by sea and largely in British ships.

On the eve of the First World War, the merchant fleet of Great Britain amounted to some 19 million gross tons of shipping, roughly 8,500 ships of over 3,000 tons. To these totals a further 1,500 ships of roughly 1,600,000 tons were owned in the Dominions, largely in Canada which possessed the world's fourth largest mercantile marine. All these vessels, whether they were registered in London or Hong Kong, Halifax, Nova Scotia, or Sydney, New South Wales, flew the British red ensign; this had become so common a sight that it was disparagingly known as 'the red duster'.

Although exclusively the ensign of the privately owned vessels of the nation's mercantile fleet since 1864, when the Royal Navy abandoned its use, it was about to become again a battle-flag of importance.

The life-line is firm
thanks to the
MERCHANT NAVY

BRITAIN'S LIFELINES

THE FIRST WORLD WAR

On the outbreak of war in 1914 Britain not only operated the largest mercantile marine in the world, she also possessed the largest navy. The Royal Navy's main battle-fleet operated out of Scapa Flow in the Orkney Islands from where it dominated the North Sea, effectively neutralising the German High Seas Fleet. Despite the appalling slaughter on the Western Front it was this sea-power which, by maintaining a blockade of Germany's short coastline, led to the collapse of the enemy, starving out its population, eroding the morale of its armed forces and eventually leading to collapse and surrender. Despite the High Seas Fleet fighting several gallant fleet actions in which they inflicted heavy losses on the Royal Navy, it was the latter that held the field, ensuring the final victory. This, however, was by no means certain, because the Germans pursued a very effective war on trade, using naval cruisers operating as far away as the South Pacific, and disguised merchantmen which had the outward appearance of harmless cargo vessels, but were actually heavily armed and manned. They also employed U-boats – an entirely new weapon.

To combat these threats in distant waters the Royal Navy attempted to patrol the trade routes of the world. It was assumed that such was the size of the British mercantile marine that while the enemy might attack it, it was too large to be seriously affected. Besides, with the new-fangled wireless, merchant ships could call for help and enemy commerce-raiders could be rapidly run down and destroyed. Other measures, such as off-setting their tracks 80 to 100 miles from the norm, would, it was thought, foil the predators. Unfortunately, many British merchant ships, many of which were still large sailing vessels, did not carry wireless transmitters and it did not take long for the Germans to work out that ships would be found running parallel to, if some scores of miles off, their traditional routes. Moreover, all ships had to converge on their destinations and loci such as the approaches to the Clyde between Scotland and Ulster, and the great triangle of the south-western approaches between Cape Clear in southern Ireland, Land's End and Ushant

Opposite:
The heroic image of the Merchant Navy at war fostered by the government emphasised the vital importance of the work being done by the civilian service. This was to counter a loss of morale among merchant seamen fostered by public ignorance of their contribution to the war effort.

29

A merchant vessel serving as a troop ship. The band plays for the Scots Guards as they board her at Southampton en route to the Western Front in France.

A German commerce-raider, a German warship disguised as a merchant vessel. This one, *Prinz Eitel Friedrich*, photographed in 1915, sank eight merchant ships.

off the Breton coast, proved a fruitful killing ground for German submarines. Although German U-boats lacked the bases in Norway and France that they would enjoy in the Second World War, they nevertheless operated in the Bay of Biscay and with great success in the Mediterranean, where Austrian submarines were also active.

First World War German U-boat built by Blohm & Voss, photographed in 1917.

The combined effect of the enemy's war on trade was severe. Losses of tonnage rose alarmingly. The traditional counter-strategy to such a *guerre de course* was, of course, to shepherd and guard a number of merchant ships in orderly convoys. This had been a war-winning tactic during the eighteenth century but by 1914 it was considered outmoded. In 1872 the Admiralty had abandoned the Compulsory Convoy Act of 1794, ignoring the introduction of the submarine to the world's navies thirty years later. Convoy was a tedious business and not one proper to an aggressive fighting navy. Nor, to their shame, did the generality of ship-owners insist upon it, as their forebears had done. The arguments against convoy in 1914 were complex but they sprang from all sectors and were largely based from the naval perspective on a lack of desire to undertake it, and from the mercantile viewpoint as inhibiting and damaging to self-interest.

Thus the globally spread ships of the mercantile marine were exposed not only to the enemy's cruisers and commerce-raiders in distant waters, but his U-boats in the western approaches and, to make matters worse, minefields in the shallow waters of the home coast, above which the Zeppelin and aircraft were now an added danger. The consequence of all this was a mounting loss of ships, cargoes and seafarers. Many ship owners and their shareholders

A rare photograph showing a British merchant vessel sinking – despite being painted with dazzle camouflage – having been struck by a German U-boat torpedo in 1917.

Merchant crewmen on a ship struck by a German U-boat in 1915. The ship manages to struggle to port with decks awash and nearly sinking.

Survivors of a merchant vessel that was sunk in the Atlantic by a U-boat in 1917.

congratulated themselves on this, making fortunes from insurance paid on lost ships, marking a dark hour of our maritime history, but so it was. Meanwhile, the merchant seaman, shivering in his lifeboat endured an unpaid ordeal – because in many cases his pay stopped the moment his ship was sunk. His drowned shipmate often got the better bargain.

For a while the balance sheet was not entirely drawn up in the enemy's favour. Two merchant captains were awarded Victoria Crosses for their actions against German raiders, though they had to be posthumously gazetted sub-lieutenants in the Royal Naval Reserve to qualify for the award. But many merchantmen, most of which had been swiftly armed with guns on their sterns for self-defence, outran or outfought U-boats addicted to surface attack, and even occasionally sank them.

The Prize Laws of the Hague Convention ruled that an enemy merchantman might only be sunk after she had been stopped and her crew removed to 'a place of safety'. Unfortunately the Hague Convention's place of safety did not exist in either a lifeboat or aboard an operational U-boat, while the Admiralty's counter-measure of commandeering merchant ships as decoys – better known as Q-ships – made of every British merchantman a potential Q-ship.

Under this threat German U-boats changed tactics; they submerged to attack with torpedoes against which there was no defence while a few German commanders perpetrated unforgivable cruelties and manifested signs of real sadism. Arguments as to whether merchantmen should be armed, even for self-defence when manned by non-combatants, lay at the heart of this, but so too did the knowledge among the U-boat crews that the British blockade was causing intense hardship to their families back in the Fatherland.

Mercantile Marine War Medal awarded to merchant seamen for one or more voyages during a war zone between 1914 and 1918. The reverse of the bronze medal shows a merchant ship sailing through stormy seas with a sinking U-boat.

We risk our lives to bring you food. It's up to you not to waste it.

'A Message from our Seamen'

A First World War poster featuring a merchant seaman, 1917, drawing attention to the role of the Merchant Navy in keeping wartime Britain supplied with food.

Nevertheless, on the British side, by the spring of 1917 the totals of lost tonnage, life and *matériel* had so reduced stocks of essentials – particularly of grain – that the Admiralty confessed to the government that they were losing the war at sea. A date was set beyond which the country could not be expected to hold out and as Russia, torn apart by Revolution, bowed out of the war, many thought that enough was enough and an honourable peace should be negotiated.

Although the new Prime Minister, David Lloyd George, took the credit, others prompted the decision to introduce convoy in the early summer of 1917. Additional measures such as the formation of a Ministry of Shipping, the effective requisition of the entire merchant fleet, the ordering of standard classes of replacement tonnage in Canada and the United States, and indeed the entry of America into the war, also had their effect – but convoy was the key. The consequences were dramatic. From the brink of capitulation, Great Britain was saved by the simple expedient of reviving a time-honoured practice – that of protecting her merchant shipping in convoy.

Firemen shovelling coal in the boiler room of a ship in 1918.

Although the Royal Navy possessed few escorts and anti-submarine warfare was primitive, Anglo-French co-operation produced sonar and a primitive form of depth-charge. Small warships and a number of naval auxiliaries were garnered as escorts, augmented in the Atlantic by American and in the Mediterranean by Japanese men-of-war. For their part merchant ships performed better in close company than their critics had presumed. Within months Germany was on her knees, her navy mutinous and her front line on the Western Front crumbling.

While economically blockading Germany, the Royal Navy had until 1917 failed to protect Britain's vital supply lines and came close – very close indeed – to losing the war. Moreover, in order to implement its own war aims, the Royal Navy had to requisition about 4,000 vessels and some 50,000 officers and ratings from the merchant marine and the fishing fleets. Fishing vessels and gentlemen's steam yachts became auxiliary patrol-craft, minesweepers and later convoy escorts; cross-Channel ferries provided ambulance transports; passenger liners became hospital ships and troopers; cargo-liners acted as transports and armed boarding vessels; and intermediate cargo-passenger liners, converted to armed merchant cruisers, either patrolled the trade routes of the world, or maintained the crucial Northern Blockade as members of the 10th Cruiser Squadron.

Some of these requisitioned merchantmen became fully commissioned naval men-of-war. Crew members in key positions, such as engineers and firemen, were retained for their expertise and thus became naval personnel under special arrangements agreed between the Admiralty and the Board

The shattered bridge of the armed liner *Carmania*, hit by enemy shells. Several Cunard ocean liners were converted to warships in the First World War, including the *Carmania*. She clashed with an armed German liner in the West Indies in 1914, which she proceeded to sink.

War memorial to the dead of the Merchant Navy and fishing fleets who gave their lives between 1914 and 1918. Sited in Tower Hill, London, it is a vaulted corridor that contains 12,000 names engraved on bronze panels. It was designed by Sir Edwin Lutyens and opened by Queen Mary in 1928.

of Trade. This was known as the T124 Agreement, allowing officers and ratings to serve in a temporary capacity in the Royal Naval Reserve (RNR) while preserving certain rates of pay and pension rights. There were some anomalies, of which the fishing skipper's metamorphosis into a Skipper RNR marks one end of the spectrum. Less happily at the other were the captains of large liners who were commissioned into the RNR but compelled to hand their ships over to naval post-captains and become their own ships' navigators. At least one liner was lost in consequence of the friction caused by this unhappy arrangement. Other requisitioned ships flew the blue ensign of transports and supporting auxiliaries, such as fleet oilers or store ships and, in time, as the Royal Navy began to appreciate the mercantile marine's virtues, many were left in the hands of their own masters with no ill effect. Meanwhile, of course, large numbers of officers and ratings of the various naval reserves had been swept up to serve in the fleet itself.

THE 'MERCHANT NAVY' AND THE GREAT DEPRESSION

From the foregoing it is clear to see that, without the supply of essential foodstuffs and raw materials to the national economy and war-effort, and without the direct support of merchant ships and seamen to the Royal Navy itself, the war could not have been won. It was therefore no surprise that when it was all over King George V spoke so enthusiastically of '*My* Merchant Navy', almost reviving the prerogative of the medieval and Tudor kings. There

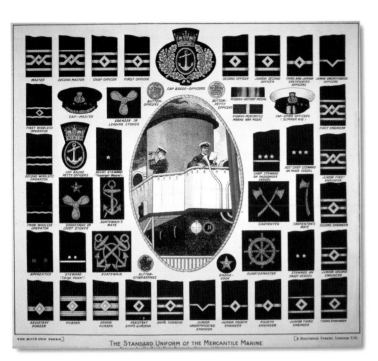

The Standard Uniform of the Mercantile Marine

Uniforms and insignia of Britain's Mercantile Marine, drawn for the *Boy's Own Paper* by Captain V. Wheeler-Holohan, *c.* 1920.

Captain F.C. Hunter wears the new uniform introduced for the Merchant Navy in 1920 with the company cap-badge of Messrs Stephenson Clarke, the collier owners for whom he worked after the First World War. In addition to his war service medals, he also sports the unusual insignia of a torpedoed mariner.

were even those who spoke of a 'Royal Merchant Navy', though this soon faded, leaving the more pragmatic 'Merchant Navy' as the new term by which the privately owned fleets of the British Empire were increasingly known.

The loss of shipping during the war ensured there was a brief post-war boom but this was not greatly to the benefit of British shipping, providing opportunities for foreign competitors whose merchant fleets had not suffered comparable attrition. It was a significant change, for it was the beginning of a slow decline in the British ownership of merchant tonnage. This was not readily apparent at the time, for the post-war boom was followed by a bust, and then the long weary years of the global Depression that followed the Wall Street crash of 1929. The shipping bust precipitated a strike among some merchant seamen in 1925, echoed in the Royal Navy in 1931 when a cut in naval pay caused a mutiny in the Atlantic Fleet at Invergordon. Many shipping companies went to the wall and the enormous Royal Mail conglomerate headed by Lord Kylsant was rescued only by the prodigious efforts of

Map showing British Empire shipping in 1937. Despite the impact of the Great Depression, trade routes were still busy with British merchant vessels.

others, Kylsant himself serving a short term in prison for issuing a false prospectus. Everywhere trade stagnated and in consequence shipbuilding came to a virtual standstill. Construction of the large new Cunarder, Ship No. 534, at John Brown's Clydebank yard was stopped until the government stepped in, compelling Cunard to merge with the White Star Line as a condition of financial help. Ship No. 534 was finally launched by George V's consort and named *Queen Mary* in her honour. Meanwhile over 40,000 merchant seamen, from masters to boys, tramped the bleak streets in search of work. It was not unusual in the early 1930s to find qualified officers, even master mariners, accepting positions as able seamen just to feed themselves and their families.

THE SECOND WORLD WAR

This began to change with the rise of Nazi Germany and the need to re-arm; international trade began to pick up and some shipping companies cautiously invested in new tonnage. However, this was barely adequate when war came again in 1939. Although the Merchant Navy rapidly found itself mustered in convoys, it was revealed that the Royal Navy had largely ignored anti-submarine warfare training during the inter-war years. Little progress had been made since 1918 and despite the protection of hurriedly assembled naval convoy escorts, the attrition rate among merchant seamen as a result of the attacks of German U-boats rose rapidly. Despite these difficulties, a convoy system with its assembly ports in Nova Scotia and West Africa, worked well, but it took the government some time to reconcile the competing demands of logistics and supply, both for the nation's war aims and its economy. In due course these problems were reconciled by amalgamating a number of ministries into the Ministry of War Transport under the remarkable Frederick (later Lord) Leathers, a protégé of Churchill's.

Although Churchill obtained the assistance of President Roosevelt of the United States to assist with the supply of armaments under the Lend-Lease agreement, it must not be forgotten that in order to pay for the war, British industry had to maintain its peacetime economic activity as far as was possible, as well as supplying munitions, guns, tanks and ammunition to the armed forces. All this vastly complicated the work of British shipping, which continued carrying exported manufactured goods as well as importing raw materials for industry and armament production. This was exacerbated after the Fall of France in the summer of 1940 and the evacuation of the British Expeditionary Force from Dunkirk. Although many thousands of British and French troops were withdrawn by vessels of both the Royal and Merchant Navies, all heavy equipment was left behind, making the re-armament of the British home army a priority. Demand was further

An aerial photograph of an Atlantic convoy heading for Great Britain in 1943. The convoy system, so successful in the First World War, was revived for the 1939–45 conflict.

Merchant ships and warships assembling at the beginning of a convoy across the Atlantic in 1943. Painting by Frank H. Mason for wartime publication.

Following spread: An attack on a merchant convoy by German aircraft, 1943. Also by Frank H. Mason for wartime publication.

increased when, in June 1941, the Germans attacked their ally, the Soviet Union. Taken by surprise the Russians fell back and Churchill, no friend of the Communist regime of Joseph Stalin, promised as much help as he could provide. This involved both the Royal and Merchant Navies in an entirely new campaign, forcing supplies round German-occupied Norway, from which the Luftwaffe and the Kriegsmarine could operate with impunity, through the icy waters of the Barents Sea to reach the ports of North Russia. During the summer months cargoes could be discharged in Archangel, but once the winter closed in only the ice-free port of Murmansk was open. As this was close to the front line the merchant ships were almost helpless as they landed their essential cargoes and endured wave after wave of aerial attack.

Despite the rapid expansion of the Royal Canadian Navy and the entry of the United States into the war after the Japanese attacked Pearl Harbor in December 1941, by the winter of 1942–3 it appeared that the sinking of ships by U-boats on the North Atlantic would cut the vital transatlantic lifeline. A number of German U-boat commanders proved adept at avoiding destruction by the inadequate defensive measures taken by the Allied naval forces escorting convoys, while the winter proved exceptionally foul across that bleak and unforgiving ocean. However, by the early spring of 1943 a number of factors began to turn the tide in the Allies' favour. Tremendous efforts had been made on both sides of the Atlantic to construct easily assembled standard merchant ships, of which the American-built 'Liberty ship' is the best example. These began to provide a steady stream of replacements for lost ships. Meanwhile, the Allied navies had also greatly improved sonar and the training of operators which, with the provision of radar and the proper development of co-ordinated anti-submarine tactics, radically improved convoy defence. More and better anti-submarine frigates were being built to supplement the hurriedly built corvettes, while other assets such as small escort aircraft carriers also began to appear in the North Atlantic and the Barents Sea.

Throughout this difficult period the losses of merchant ships and their vital cargoes had threatened the British with defeat. Aboard the sorely tried merchantmen the average merchant seaman had suffered a long loss of esteem. Although many officers wore uniform at sea, few did so ashore, while the seamen, firemen and stewards had no uniform and were often shunned by people ashore who thought they were conscientious objectors. While the general population went through the so-called 'Phoney War' the merchant sailor was being sunk and consigned to the cold sea only to reach shore often with little on his back, his pay stopped and his welcome insulting. The government introduced an enamel lapel badge and launched a propaganda campaign which sought proper acknowledgement of the Merchant

A German U-boat shells a merchant vessel, as depicted in a wartime painting by H. R. Butler.

The armed British merchant steamer *Highlander* brings down two German aircraft. (Front page of *The War Weekly*, 1940.)

A Royal Navy convoy escort launches depth charges at a German U-boat during the Battle of the Atlantic.

Navy's essential but unglamorous contribution to the war effort. It bore the initials 'M.N.' which many seafarers turned upside down, meaning 'N.W.' for 'Not Wanted.' Matters came to a head in the summer of 1942 when the Russia-bound convoy PQ17 was dispersed on Admiralty orders. Having assumed that the convoy was about to be attacked by the German battleship *Tirpitz* and a flotilla of destroyers, the Admiralty instructed its main ocean escort to withdraw to the westward and cover its dispersal. In fact the decision was made on faulty intelligence and the convoy was destroyed piecemeal by U-boats and aircraft. It was an unfortunate blunder, an inescapable consequence of the 'fog of war', but it fed the merchant seaman's paranoia and led to years of post-war hostility to the Royal Navy which was, quite unfairly, thought to have 'run away'.

This was the nadir of the merchant seaman's war; British and Allied merchant ships continued to be sunk all over the world, not just by German U-boats in the North Atlantic, but as far away as the Cape of Good Hope, while the Japanese made their own bloody contribution, even sinking a fully illuminated hospital ship, the *Centaur*. In the event, proportional to the numbers engaged, a merchant seaman had a lesser chance of survival than his brother in the armed services.

Nevertheless, although the German submarine offensive was renewed in September 1943, it was never again to enjoy the successes of the war's early years. Many convoys passed across the North Atlantic without an alarm and notions of the ocean 'swarming' with U-boats were inaccurate. Certainly fierce battles were fought round a significant number of convoys – the Germans' U-boat base at L'Orient in western France helped them, whilst other bases in occupied Norway were able to operate against Russia-bound convoys – but the Allied improvements in technical equipment, the increased numbers of merchant and naval forces, combined with the bombing offensive against German industry, began to wear down the enemy. Although the Germans worked hard to counter many of these advantages, they had lost the initiative, while the quality of U-boat crews, faced with increasing losses at sea (including either the death or capture of several of their aces), deteriorated with time.

The planned Allied invasion of Vichy French North Africa required large numbers of merchant ships as auxiliaries, including many liners which operated as large landing craft, capable of launching small flat-bottomed boats able to convey an infantry brigade ashore. Other merchantmen fulfilled sundry special tasks as the Allied forces gained experience in amphibious

Merchant vessels arrive at Malta after convoy through the Mediterranean in 1943. (Painting by Frank H. Mason for wartime publication.)

A wartime painting of munitions and weapons being unloaded from a merchant vessel in a British dock after surviving convoy from the US across the Atlantic.

landings in Madagascar, Syria, Sicily, Italy and finally Normandy on D-Day, 6 June 1944.

Although Nazi Germany collapsed eleven months later, the war against the Japanese went on for some months. British shipping had been caught up

The Second World War memorial to 24,000 dead from the merchant marine, set in a sunken garden at Tower Hill, London. It was opened by Queen Elizabeth II in 1955.

throughout the aggressive years of the Sino-Japanese War which had begun in 1937. The Japanese occupation of Hong Kong, Malaya, Singapore and Borneo had caused heavy casualties of ships and men, many of the latter being Chinese seamen employed aboard British ships. Indeed, multi-nationality was a feature of the crews of a very large number of British merchant ships, as an inspection of the Merchant Navy War Memorial in the gardens of London's Tower Hill will testify.

Sculptures of a merchant marine officer (*left*) and seaman (*right*) at the Tower Hill Second World War memorial, designed by Charles Wheeler.

Even today, few outside the families of those directly affected really appreciate the contribution made by merchant seafarers to final Allied victory, despite the institution of Merchant Navy Day on 3 September 2000. This is best illustrated by the continuing refusal at the time of writing (2012) of the government to grant a separate campaign medal to those who took part in the convoys to North Russia between 1941 and 1945. For the Merchant Navy the Second World War began on the first day of hostilities, 3 September 1939, when the passenger liner *Athenia* was torpedoed off Northern Ireland by *U-30*, and lasted until 7 May 1945, the same day that Germany surrendered unconditionally at Rheims, when the *Avondale Park* was sunk in the Firth of Forth by *U-2336*.

The Atlantic Star campaign medal was awarded to merchant seamen as well as navy personnel for six months' service afloat between 1939 and 1945 in Atlantic home waters, the North Russian convoys or South Atlantic waters.

LIFE AT SEA

EXHAUSTED BY WAR, the British Merchant Navy had to adjust to a diminished role in the post-war world. The United States of America had become the pre-eminent sea-power as Britain's colonies gained independence in the succeeding decades. The new government denied British ships the coastal routes they had once enjoyed, establishing their own merchant fleets while many young cadets from former colonies were trained in traditional British companies –though most received scant thanks. Meanwhile, a new threat arose from those countries secured by

A steam coaster owned by Monroe Brothers of Glasgow crosses Mount's Bay and heads for the Lizard. Painted by Gordon Ellis in 1962, it is the type of vessel described by John Masefield in his poem 'Cargoes' as a 'dirty British coaster with a salt-caked smoke stack, butting up the Channel in a mad March gale.'

Soviet Russia behind the 'Iron Curtain'. Encouraged by the Stalinist instrument formed as the Council for Mutual Economic Assistance, or 'Comecon', aggressive shipbuilding produced new fleets of merchantmen able to compete unfairly on the open market.

British ship-owners nevertheless began to make good their war losses, though British shipyards failed to embrace new techniques, leading eventually to their decline in the face of foreign competition. Although British shipping carried a much smaller proportion of the world's commodities, the years between 1945 and 1970 are regarded by many as a 'golden age' when conditions at sea were good, pay was adequate and a future seemed assured. Many young men went to sea in this period, some going first to a pre-sea school to earn remission from sea-time as cadets and apprentices before sitting for their formal qualifications. Some went directly from school, aged sixteen; others went as deck- or galley-boys at fifteen and, since the Merchant Navy remained a meritocracy, could rise to the highest command. Young women went to sea as stewardesses or assistant pursers; later women entered the executive and engineering departments, becoming master-mariners and chief engineers. Occasionally a company would identify a bright young man or woman and they would enter shore management, several reaching board level.

In these years cargo ships spent roughly one day in port for every one or two at sea. Shore leave was usually granted and time ashore was spent according to the individual's enterprise. Many got no further than the bars along the waterfront; some made cultural trips inland; and most enjoyed the hospitality offered by the Mission to Seamen,

Midshipman John Hunter on the boat-deck of one of Alfred Holt's Blue Funnel liners in the early 1960s. He wears a blazer badge of the naval crown – symbolic of a national Merchant Navy.

A consortium of four British shipping companies established Overseas Containers Ltd. to serve traditional routes to the Far East and Australia. Their first container ship left Europe on 6 March 1969, and the second generation, of which the *Osaka Bay* was one, entered service in the 1970s. These ships were no longer defined by tonnage, but by the number of 'twenty-foot equivalent units', or teu, that they could carry. The *Osaka Bay*'s 2,961 teu has long been superseded.

the Apostleship of the Sea or the British Sailors' Society, which had premises worldwide. Life was very different in tankers with loading and discharging times kept to a minimum and the oil terminals miles from any flesh-pots. While the life at sea depended upon the resources of the individual, this was particularly true of tanker men. Off-duty time at sea was absorbed by studying, sun-bathing or sleeping, for exams had to be passed by those aiming for an officer's job. Makeshift swimming pools were erected during passages of more than a few days in those vessels trading in the tropics, such amenities being commonplace fixtures in many larger passenger liners.

Conditions of employment during these halcyon post-war years steadily improved. Although never excessively remunerated, seafarers were able to provide a modest living for wives and families. Officers and ratings still signed on and off the Articles of Agreement on a voyage-by-voyage basis; this might be a month at a time, or in a tramp ship the full two-year term, during which the minimum in pay and food as established by the Board of Trade (or any of its successors – today the Maritime and Coastguard Agency) was the seaman's lot. Better conditions, but the same two-year stretch, might also be encountered in a cargo-liner engaged in a foreign cross-trade. With such a variety of opportunities the life suited many, promising as it did a career structure. Certificates of Competency for both the navigating (deck) and engineering disciplines – commonly known as 'tickets' – required a short course of study followed by formal examination at the Board of Trade's offices

View of the wheelhouse on the bridge of the *Canberra*, a P&O passenger liner in operation from 1961 to 1997. Built in Belfast, she was one of the merchant vessels that sailed with the British fleet in 1982 in the Falklands War, where she acted as a troop ship.

An officer studies the radar display on the bridge of the *Canberra*. Withdrawn from service in 1997, the *Canberra* was sold for scrap to ship breakers in Pakistan.

in any of the larger ports. Consisting of written papers and oral examination they could prove an ordeal testing the most able of candidates.

For most, however, in those pre-air-travel days, a few years at sea assuaged a desire to 'see the world' and seafaring was an essentially young man's calling. Wastage was around sixty per cent but gradual improvements in social conditions ashore and an increasing desire for self-expression eroded any advantages seafaring might have had to prevent a lad from 'going down the pit' or working on an assembly line. Moreover, the sexual liberation of the 1960s began to make the life less attractive as marriages failed.

The ability to take one's holidays abroad, and to do so by air, began to shift seafaring out of the public mind. As industrial troubles tore apart the shipyards and the docks, ship owners attempted to initiate large British container consortia, but these failed to flourish and even the ship owners began to seek investment in other industries. Despite a last hurrah with the chartering of over fifty merchantmen to assist the Task Force sent to recapture the Falkland Islands in 1982, it was clear that Britain's traditional Merchant Navy was in decline.

NEW CHALLENGES

A TTEMPTS to reverse this decline were made during Blair's New Labour ministry when John Prescott, MP for the former fishing port of Hull and himself a sometime steward at sea, introduced the Tonnage Tax regime mentioned earlier. This, it will be recalled, enabled ships to be registered in the United Kingdom and fly the red ensign. The high standards of compliance this entailed placed such owners on the so-called 'white list' of international shipping-registries, implying good governance and high safety standards. However, few such owners registering their ships in Great Britain in the early years of the twenty-first century were actually British, and in a globalised industry the red ensign has begun to look very much like a flag of opportunity, if not of convenience.

The decline in British-owned and manned shipping is complex, influenced by a lack of investment, which ensured British shipbuilding failed to keep pace with foreign competition. The exasperation of many owners was exacerbated by dock labour disputes and in 1966 the National Union of Seamen called its members out on a damaging strike. The attempt to form a large British consortium to embrace the new integrated containerised transport system three years later was marred from the start when the first British container ship, the German-built *Encounter Bay*, was compelled to load at Rotterdam, not London. Despite the heavy investment of four major

The roll-on, roll-off cargo vessel *Eddystone* is owned by Foreland Shipping, a consortium formed in 2001 by four British shipping companies to provide the British Government with strategic sealift capacity. Of the six ships involved, two are usually on charter to the Government with the remaining four on short notice to be taken up from trade should the need arise.

52

British ship-owners, the enterprise was ultimately frustrated. Less troublesome investments attracted many ship owners, while the traditional ties with distant members of the Commonwealth were cut in favour of the European trading community, only a short distance away, through the brand-new Channel Tunnel.

Consequent anxieties about national security led to an expansion of the Royal Fleet Auxiliary at the tax-payers' expense, although a number of vessels are run by Foreland Shipping on the understanding that the state has an option on their chartering if required. It is difficult to see these arrangements, or the variable number of foreign-owned but British-flagged merchantmen currently at sea, as a 'Merchant Navy' in the way in which the term was conceived; 'mercantile marine' is – once again – the more fitting term.

The country still requires men and women trained to the sea; schemes, supported by charities like Trinity House, exist for the promotion of cadetships and the encouragement of subsequent careers at sea and in the maritime infrastructure ashore. Whatever its future fortunes, UK plc will require men and women whose understanding of sea transport and trade enable it – and us – to remain competitive and thrive. We remain an island nation, dependent on shipping for economic survival; 95 per cent of our imports still arrive on our shores by sea. In this respect nothing has changed.

Globalisation of trade has shifted the heart of the merchant marine away from Europe to Asia and ports such as Singapore.

PLACES TO VISIT

MUSEUMS

Discovery Museum, Blandford Square, Newcastle upon Tyne NE1 4JA.
Telephone: 0191 232 6789.
Website: www.twmuseums.org.uk/discovery

Merseyside Maritime Museum, Albert Dock, Liverpool Waterfront, Liverpool L3 4AQ.
Telephone: 0151 478 4499.
Website: www.liverpoolmuseums.org.uk/maritime

National Maritime Museum, Park Row, Greenwich SE10 9NF.
Telephone 020 8858 4422. Website: www.rmg.co.uk

Scottish Maritime Museum has two sites: Linthouse Building, Harbour Road, Irvine, Ayrshire KA12 8QE (telephone: 01294 278283); Denny Ship Model Experiment Tank, Castle Street, Dumbarton G82 1QS (telephone: 01389 763 444).
Website: www.scottishmaritimemuseum.org

Tower Hill Memorial, Trinity Square, Tower Hill, London. Memorial Register held at Trinity House Corporation, Trinity Square (Cooper's Row entrance), Tower Hill, London EC3N 4DH.
Telephone: 020 7481 6900.

SHIPS

Cutty Sark (clipper), King William Walk, Greenwich, London SE10 9HT.
Telephone: 020 8858 4422.
Website: www.rmg.co.uk

Glenlee (barque), The Tall Ship at Riverside, 150 Pointhouse Place, Glasgow G3 8RS. Telephone: 0141 357 3699.
Website: www.thetallship.com

Great Britain (Brunel's masterpiece), Great Western Dockyard, Bristol BS1 6TY.
Telephone: 0117 926 0680.
Website: www.ssgreatbritain.org

Kathleen and May (schooner), Bideford, Devon.
Website: www.kathleenandmay.co.uk

Robin (steam coaster), Visitor Centre, 2D/2E Royal Victoria Place, London E16 1UQ. Reopens in 2013. Telephone 0207 998 1343.
Website: www.ssrobin.com

Shieldhall (working steamship), Berth 48, Dock Gate 4, Ocean Dock, Southampton. Telephone: 07751 603190.
Website: www.ss-shieldhall.co.uk

FURTHER READING

Artmonsky, Ruth. *P&O: A History*. Shire Publications, 2012.

Falkus, Malcolm. *The Blue Funnel Legend*. Palgrave Macmillan, 1990.

Hope, Ronald. *A New History of British Shipping*. J. Murray, 1990.

Howarth, David and Stephen. *The Story of P&O*. Weidenfeld & Nicolson, 1994.

Lane, Tony. *Grey Dawn Breaking: British Merchant Seafarers in the Late Twentieth Century*. Manchester University Press, 1986.

Woodman, Richard. *Fiddler's Green* (A History of the British Merchant Navy, Volume 5). The History Press, 2010.

Woodman, Richard. *The Real Cruel Sea: The Merchant Navy in the Battle of the Atlantic, 1939–1943*. Pen and Sword Maritime, 2011.

INDEX